PSYCHOLOGY OF MONEY AND PROPENSITY

The Mindset of Creating Abundance

Judy Theodorah

DEDICATION

I Dedicate this book to God Almighty, for successful publishing.
Also to those that make this book a reality, thanks so much.

CONTENTS

CHAPTER 1

INVESTIGATING PROPENSITIES AND HOW THEY WORK

Propensity is a procured way of behaving routinely followed until it has become nearly involuntary. This implies that a propensity is a way of behaving that is more than once finished until you nearly don't realize that you are in any event, making it happen. It becomes like natural to you.

Subsequently, this inside and out concentrate on lets us know two vital things:

• Propensities don't become programmed for the time being

• Propensities can't be broken for the time being.

A propensity is something that main comes by means of time and rehashed activity. We frequently don't perceive ourselves as doing a negative behavior pattern until generally another person focuses it out. The cerebrum likes to foster these propensities since it can monitor its psychological energy toward one more undertaking while it takes part in the propensity Beneficial routines Versus Unfortunate behavior patterns In the middle of Between.

In truth, the main genuine contrast among great and persistent vices is that the gained way of behaving is a decent activity or a shocking act as characterized by most of society.

• You want to figure out what positive routines you need to take on, then, at that point, rehash the great activity that comprises that propensity over and again until you do it naturally without acknowledging it.

• You want to perceive the negative behavior patterns you need to abrogate, then try not to rehash the atrocity that comprises that propensity ceaselessly until you consequently do an elective activity rather that is viewed as better compared to that heinous act.

It will require investment to "revamp" your cerebrum to discard the persistent vice and take up the new positive routine. Activities that require more exertion will find opportunity to embrace as propensities contrasted with those activities that require less exertion.

Characterize Vices And Stage Them Out Of Your Life, Unfortunate behavior patterns are ways of behaving thought about awful by the vast majority of society and are more than once finished by the person.We become so resistant to the activity since it appears to be so normal to us that others for the most part need to direct out the activity toward us. Bringing an end to or superseding the vice won't be a short-term process, and contingent upon rapidly you embrace new propensities and the intricacy of the action(s) involved, could require half a month to a while to take on the new propensity.

Step by Step Instructions to Frame Beneficial Routines and Make Them Stick

At the point when you have a vice and need to supplant it with a positive routine, you really want to deliberately know about the negative behavior pattern and understand what activity you want to change to transform the vice into the beneficial routine.

• We really want to figure out what elective move we should make to wipe out the horrendous act.

• We should rehash the positive activity often previously it will become imbued in our activities and we begin doing this new way of behaving consequently without acknowledging it.This is the point at which the persistent vice will be eradicated and the positive routine is laid out.

Set Up An Emotionally supportive network To Remain focused

It's very conceivable you will do the old negative behavior pattern various times while attempting to incorporate the new positive routine to supersede the persistent vice.

• An emotionally supportive network can be useful in guaranteeing you keep focused into coordinating the new propensity into your normal everyday practice.

• An emotionally supportive network can incorporate loved ones who can monitor you and guarantee you're staying with the new positive routine.

• An emotionally supportive network can incorporate a memory gadget, like tying a piece of string around your pointer, to remind you to do the great activity/conduct, not the shocking act/conduct.

Begin Little And Make Abundance Each New Propensity In turn

The vast majority will endeavor to roll out monstrous improvements to their lives rather than attempting to simplify one change.The issue with the enormous change approach is that individuals frequently attempt to do excessively, get overpowered, lose inspiration and excitement for it, then, at that point, return to their old propensities and routines.It's smarter to effectively incorporate another propensity as opposed to attempting to execute 3-5 new propensities and just doing them periodically, while as yet doing your old propensities to a great extent.

• How much exertion expected to effectively carry out another propensity will straightforwardly affect what amount of time it requires to execute that new propensity effectively.

• To embrace is complicated and significant, you ought to hope to carve out opportunity to incorporate it into your standard routine effectively.

Each new propensity you need to coordinate into your normal routine is something you accept will assist you with working on your life and create your financial stability, however that won't occur in the event that you don't effectively incorporate it.Take the expected time important to guarantee that another propensity is effectively incorporated into your daily practice. Doing the positive routine half of the time and the unfortunate behavior pattern half of the time truly doesn't significantly benefit you for certain, nor work on your life and riches. Wash, Rehash And Keep up with New

Propensities.

Brady work won't prompt the open door you thought, you're in charge to leave. You're likewise in charge to continue on for one more month and remain until everybody's more agreeable and the kimono possibly opens up. You're in charge. You're in charge of thinking about this as a postulation - very much like individuals who are unyielding that I'm a trouble maker or that this flawed guidance. I'm compassionate to them. In any case, I'm no more "right" than they are. For the people that read this book you get to choose.

The trashing of free work or spec turn out is great, it's simply something that I know huge number of individuals have used to turn out to find success. Furthermore, those are only individuals I am aware of - and that implies numerous a lot more have. Individuals say that the ones who can accomplish free work are special - I contend that the ones who battle against it are favored and don't understand the number of individuals that would very much like a way in. Those individuals who battle against it don't understand the number of individuals that can never have a chance, and the forceful, innovative thought of "I'll show you" is precisely how individuals who could never have had a shot really begun the method involved with having the chance.

CHAPTER 2

HERE IS THE TRUTH OF KARMA

I've found that the harder I work the more fortunate I get. In the event that you need command over your predetermination and to have your results under your influence however much as could be expected, you must get off your duff and accomplish the work important to get it going. I've lived for fewl many years now and I've never seen karma show improvement over the technique I've recently depicted. A lot of other known and substantially more cultivated people than I concur.

Karma doesn't have anything to do with it, since I have spent many, numerous hours, endless hours, on the court working for my one second in time, not knowing when it would come. You'll be astounded at how karma will begin showing up. However, the point might be made that this isn't generally obvious: For instance, you can purposefully advance toward a game to get the signature of a headliner (not karma) and either the headliner has been harmed and will not be playing that day or there are such countless individuals in front of you that you simply never get to the star to their mark. (misfortune). This decision would be an error, not withstanding. The thing that matters is you purposefully and intentionally made the move important to get it going. A few things are only not in your control, that is not karma, it's simply an event that you had zero command over regardless of your expectations. It likewise implies you have some control over the conditions next time by verifying whether the player will be available and arriving in front of others so you can be one of the preferred choice.

Karma is summarized in the expressions of Thomas Jefferson, one of the principal architects of America. I'm'm an extraordinary devotee to karma, and I find the harder I work the more I have of it.Thomas Jefferson realize that karma never bests difficult work and commitment to arrive at an objective. God himself settles the idea that karma has bearing on results. In His Promise, He requires activity - what directs karma to cling to that idea.

You won't ever be more fortunate than the cost you're willing to pay to accomplish your goals. Luck won't assist you with eliminating the obstructions that block the way to your picked objective. Just coarseness, fortitude, and assurance to move heaven and earth, if fundamental, will do that. Luck generally is by all accounts against the individual who relies upon it. Try not to allow anyone to trick you. You can be essentially as fortunate as you need to be. Go out and get karma going something from their life and not mess up the same way.

CHAPTER 3

TWO UNIQUE ABILITIES: REMAINING RICH AND GETTING RICH

Abundance is the wealth of any significant belonging or cash. Becoming well off and remaining affluent are two distinct abilities. Morgan Housel says keeping your abundance requires something contrary to facing challenges. It requires modesty and dread that what you've made can be detracted from you similarly as quick. Remaining rich includes only a couple of straightforward things like mindfulness, unobtrusiveness, and the capacity to defer satisfaction with a part of your profit.

People tend to burn through cash on superficial points of interest. In any event, when an individual can not bear the cost of an iPhone, he would in any case get one on EMIs (Likened Regularly scheduled payments). Purchasing resources for display your abundance will just make you more unfortunate. In the event that you don't quit purchasing things you needn't bother with, you will before long need to sell things you really want. In your initial years, obligation is the most exceedingly terrible thing you can take. Compounding is viewed as the eighth marvel of the world, rather than profiting from it, individuals are becoming prey to it.

Is remaining well off actually so troublesome? Indeed, it's very inconspicuous. To begin with, you really want to comprehend that looking well off is totally unique in relation to being affluent. Altering the mentality is the initial step. Then comes taking care of your obligations, particularly the exorbitant interest ones. Next comes saving and financial planning. Saving is significant in light of the fact that realizing that you have a security net assuming you fall is calming. Also, effective financial planning, begin doing it quickly, if not, expansion will consume all your cash. Begin making present moment and long haul monetary objectives and audit them routinely.

Individuals frequently debase the worth cash brings to lives. Cash is something we consume our lives energy for, so consistently attempt to remain rich.

Procedure on the best way to contribute and develop abundance

While abundance can be acquired or, seldom, procured by karma, numerous well off people began with a little retirement fund and created their financial momentum decisively. They have utilized numerous ways of saving, put away and develop their cash — and the uplifting news is, a considerable lot of these methodologies can be taken on by us all, regardless of what level of abundance we're beginning with.

1. Not Leaving Cash Sitting Inactive

Creating genuine financial momentum requires not sitting on your cash. You hear rich people looking at the time about being cash destitute, Does it mean they are poor? No. It implies they never keep huge amounts of cash lying around torpid. It's the cash in, cash out belief system. Cash should be working for you consistently if you have any desire to arrive at the degrees of genuinely rich people.

2. Zeroing in On The 'Signal,' Not The 'Commotion'

The main propensity for rich families is keeping a hierarchical perspective on their own monetary record. They're centered around a year-over-year expansion in complete total assets, and they don't squander a lot of energy on the subtleties. They have refined experts who are dealing with the subtleties, or clamor, and who can dig profound on a case by case basis. Watching out for the sign, not the noise is significant.

3. Checking Pay And Costs

Independence from the rat race is an element of income. A decent practice is to screen types of revenue and costs reliably. On the off chance that you spend each dollar of pay on private utilization, you have no capacity to create financial stability through reserve funds and venture. It's not the amount you acquire, it's the amount you consume!

4. Esteeming Their Time

Assuming the time it takes to clean your home is more significant than the expense of getting somebody to assist you with cleaning your home, re-appropriate it. I can make $XX in the two hours it takes me to go to the supermarket, shop and return home. It will cost me $X in tips to have another person do it for me. Wiping out these interruptions likewise helps creation, in this manner further raising that worth.

5. Laying out Life Objectives And A Monetary Arrangement

One fundamental practice that is basically significant is to defined life objectives and make a monetary arrangement to meet those objectives. Remembering this arrangement as everyday choices are gained and consistently evaluating headway toward that plan is vital.

6. Utilizing Protection Decisively

The well off use protection decisively. Dissimilar to the vast majority of the populace, they don't exclusively use protection to supplant lost pay during their functioning years. The rich frequently use protection as a feature of their domain arranging, their duty procedure or even in their family banking.

7. Meeting Routinely With Their Monetary Guides

The propensity I have seen affluent individuals utilize most effectively is to meet every year (while perhaps not more regularly) with their monetary consultants to grasp their monetary world. Bookkeepers, monetary counsels and domain arranging groups are individuals who have the monetary data that permits affluent individuals to pursue better choices and grasp the condition of their funds

8. Figuring out The Duty Premise And Undiscovered Additions In Their Portfolios

One monetary propensity a considerable lot of my high-total assets clients practice is figuring out the expense premise and hidden gains in their portfolios consistently. Making the most of chances to reap charge misfortunes, in the event that the choices line up with your general venture methodology, is a simple method for guaranteeing you are never paying more duty on capital additions than is totally needed.

9. Adhering To A Spending plan

I think it begins with doing the rudiments right — and for some, that is knowing, and adhering to, a financial plan. It's not difficult to forget about where your cash is going consistently when such countless costs are set up to be paid through autopay, and nobody conveys cash, so it's not difficult to lose that feeling of what's being spent. Look at that and see what you can straighten out, or even what extra supports you can save!

10. Routinely Contributing

The rich participate in ongoing financial planning. Reliably contribute a sum that is agreeable for your conditions. With regards to financial planning, propensity and consistency are fundamental. Consider mechanizing your stores straightforwardly from your profit into your speculation account. Begin this training early, and increment your stores as your income increment. Pick a sum and recurrence that you can focus on as long as possible.

11 Laying out Short-And Long haul Objectives

Put forth practical monetary objectives, evaluate them frequently and construct an arrangement to accomplish them. Many individuals need to "resign at age x" or "save y sum by age z," yet without a substantial arrangement or comprehension of the possibility of these objectives, it's difficult to be aware in the event that you're on target to accomplish them. Everybody ought to lay out present moment and long haul objectives, track achievements and change en route on a case by case basis.

12. Bringing in Their Cash Work For Them

One individual monetary propensity rich individuals follow is to bring in certain that their cash is working "for" them. As such, set your cash to work through speculations and organizations with the goal that the cash continues to develop. Reliably recognize "lethargic cash," and set it to work.

13. Gaining Monetary Information And Abilities

The vast majority don't understand that your way of thinking about anything, including cash, controls your propensities, which perpetually decide your result. It's fitting to obtain the right monetary abilities and foster a relentless longing for monetary information. Regularly practice it to gain monetary information and abilities; then you can create an existence of manageable financial stability.

14. Facing Taught Challenges

Figure out your gamble resilience, and don't hesitate for even a moment to face instructed challenges. This standard can be applied both in business and with your ventures. It is critical to do a few exploration and encircle yourself with individuals who can take you to a higher level and assist you with pursuing an educated choice. For instance, a monetary counselor can direct you in facing gradual challenges in view of your degree of solace.

15. Try not to take part in bad self-talk.

With regards to brain research and cash, the main thing more regrettable than encircling yourself with failures is accepting you're a washout. Do you make statements like, My occupation is too intense, It's not my shortcoming, or I'm not brilliant enough. Say sufficiently that, and you'll trust it. At the point when you permit cynicism to control your contemplations, you are customizing your mind for disappointment, Corley composed. You'll get no opportunity in life at breaking out of your current monetary or life conditions. These negative contemplations will become convictions that carry on like PC programs.

16. Carry on with a sound way of life.

Bringing in cash takes resolve and work. Exercise does as well and eating right. Dealing with your funds and your wellbeing remain closely connected. Chronic weakness propensities make negative karma, Corley composed. This is a kind of karma that is a side-effect of unfortunate things to do, unfortunate way of behaving, and terrible direction. In the event that you're an animal who has in excess of several these propensities, odds are you could require help escaping obligation. A charitable obligation the board program is a demonstrated way out.

CONCLUSION

No one is great, and the key is to have more beneficial routines than awful ones. Taking on one rich habit,Corley composed, disposes of numerous unfortunate things to do. In this way, assuming that you'reunder water, quit observing such a lot of television, read more begin making arrangements, think emphatically and find additional revenue sources.